she loves me
he loves me not

Rob Ruiz & Emily Navarro

RUSTIC SOUL PUBLISHING

RUSTIC SOUL PUBLISHING
Chicago, Illinois
www.rusticsoulpublishing.com

Copyright © 2008 by RUSTIC SOUL PUBLISHING

All rights reserved. No part of this literary work may be reproduced
in any form or by any means, without the expressed written
consent of the publisher.

On file with the Library of Congress and the Writers Guild of America

ISBN: 978-0-6152-1491-7

Printed in the United States of America
Cover art by: Angel Agosto

Please send manuscripts or inquiries to:
Rustic Soul Publishing
2109 N. Spaulding Ave.
Chicago, IL. 60647
info@rusticsoulpublishing.com

For my father, Juan B. Navarro
You showed me that true love can conquer any obstacle
even death

For my Pops, Mami, Sonia, Cheo, Chanita
and three guardian angels
Alcapurrias

With a poetic style of her own, never following any traditional rules, Emily Navarro has embarked on this first time literary journey to share her feelings with the world. All of her entries are inspired and are a reflection of her own personal experiences. Always wearing her heart on her sleeve, never ashamed to express her true emotions, and always true to her own state of mind.

"I'm in love with the idea of falling in love", exclaims Emily.

Stemming from a traditional Puerto Rican family and raised in the Buck town area of Chicago, Emily delved into her writing at an early age as a way of releasing the pressures, frustrations, and roller coaster ride of emotions that were tangled up inside ready to burst. She can only hope that her words will serve their purpose of touching hearts, placing a physical sight to what others may have felt, but never dared to share, and hopeful that her words, in some way, help heal an ailing heart.

Born and raised in the then gritty Northwest side of Chicago, Rob Ruiz has seen and experienced his share of heartache and despair. With many of his childhood friends joining gangs, going to jail, and being murdered, he chose to turn to the Arts as a way to express not only his anger, frustration, and heartache, but a way to express his talent to his peers.

"Writing was not only a tool for expressing myself but a weapon against injustice in our hood", proclaims Rob.

He went on to write stage plays which cast many of the youth of the neighborhood as lead actors and screenplays that cast former gang members, as a form of community outreach.

It was during the passing of his high school sweetheart in a drunk-driving accident that his poetic voice took form and love became the topic of choice. His pain and anguish evolved into scribed fury as the months and years passed after her absence.

What you will experience in this book is raw emotion, compassion, heartbreak, desire, and the elusive nature of love.

Contents

Love – Rob Ruiz	1
Forgive Me – Rob Ruiz	2
What Am I Looking for? – Emily Navarro	3
Gone – Emily Navarro	4
The Impossible – Rob Ruiz	5
Tears of a Clown – Rob Ruiz	6
El Amor – Emily Navarro	7
Without Saying Goodbye – Rob Ruiz	8
2007 – Emily Navarro	9, 10
Why Have You Forsaken Me? – Rob Ruiz	11
Again I Cry – Emily Navarro	12
Flash Love – Rob Ruiz	13
Despierta – Emily Navarro	14
Paradise Lost – Rob Ruiz	15
Reflection – Emily Navarro	16
Daddy's Little Girl – Emily Navarro	17
I Watch While I Wait – Emily Navarro	18
Quote – Rob Ruiz	19
Repented Heart – Rob Ruiz	20
Love Lost – Rob Ruiz	21
Carry It With You – Emily Navarro	22
It's Over – Emily Navarro	23
The Journey – Rob Ruiz	24
Looking for Love – Rob Ruiz	25
Quote – Rob Ruiz	26
What Am I? – Emily Navarro	27
In Dedication of My Friend – Emily Navarro	28
Quote – Emily Navarro	29
El Espacio – Emily Navarro	30
Imagine – Rob Ruiz	31
Accidental Love – Rob Ruiz	32
Just When I Decided – Emily Navarro	33
Touch – Rob Ruiz	34
Quote – Rob Ruiz	35
It's Time – Rob Ruiz	36, 37
Lesson Learned – Emily Navarro	38

Amor – Rob Ruiz	39
Finding Him – Emily Navarro	40
You Never Knew – Emily Navarro	41
Quote – Emily Navarro	42
Soar – Rob Ruiz	43
Quote – Emily Navarro	44
Quote – Rob Ruiz	45
Heartbreak Manifesto – Rob Ruiz	46, 47
Me enamore… de el – Emily Navarro	48
Plegaria – Emily Navarro	49
Quote – Emily Navarro	50
Quote – Rob Ruiz	51
Quote – Emily Navarro	52
Listen – Rob Ruiz	53
Sacred – Rob Ruiz	54
Seasons Change – Rob Ruiz	55
Quote – Rob Ruiz	56
Invisible – Emily Navarro	57
Love Holds No Prisoners – Emily Navarro	58, 59
Quote – Rob Ruiz	60
Black Blood – Rob Ruiz	61
Deny Me?! How Dare You?! – Emily Navarro	62, 63
Suicide – Rob Ruiz	64, 65
A Consequence – Emily Navarro	66
Quote – Rob Ruiz	67
My Heart Chose You – Emily Navarro	68
Quote – Emily Navarro	69
Quote – Rob Ruiz	70
Believe In Yourself – Emily Navarro	71
Quote – Rob Ruiz	72
Seasons May Change… but the Love stays the Same – Emily Navarro	73
Quote – Rob Ruiz	74
Pillow Talk – Emily Navarro	75
Quote – Rob Ruiz	76
Distant Desire – Rob Ruiz	77, 78
Quote – Emily Navarro	79
Someday… Just Doesn't Look Like It's Gonna Be Today – Emily Navarro	80, 81

Quote – Rob Ruiz	82
Dear Love – Emily Navarro	83, 84
Quote – Rob Ruiz	85
Sparkle – Emily Navarro	86
Quote – Rob Ruiz	87
Pillow Talk – Emily Navarro	88
Eternal – Rob Ruiz	89
Quote – Emily Navarro	90
In Search of – Rob Ruiz	91
The Star to the Left of the Moon – Emily Navarro	92
The Core – Rob Ruiz	93
Myths – Emily Navarro	94
Elisa's Garden – Rob Ruiz	95
2 Seconds Until Forever – Rob Ruiz	96-102
Tired – Emily Navarro	103
Incredible You – Rob Ruiz	104
Quote – Rob Ruiz	105
Wrong Number – Emily Navarro	106, 107
Find Myself – Rob Ruiz	108
I Drink to My Heart – Emily Navarro	109
Quote – Rob Ruiz	110
Death of My Heart – Emily Navarro	111
Quote – Rob Ruiz	112
You Took – Emily Navarro	113
The Hopeful – Rob Ruiz	114
The Intimate Stranger – Rob Ruiz	115
Quote – Emily Navarro	116
Recapture – Rob Ruiz	117
Quote – Emily Navarro	118
Beginning and End – Emily Navarro	119
It Feels – Rob Ruiz	120
Everyday – Emily Navarro	121
Quote – Emily Navarro	122
Sweet Memories – Emily Navarro	123
Why Bother? – Emily Navarro	124, 125
Alphabetical Reasoning – Rob Ruiz	126
A Real Man Eats – Rob Ruiz	127
Until Death Do Us Part – Rob Ruiz	128
My Addiction – Rob Ruiz	129

Quote – Emily Navarro	130
What is Fuck? – Rob Ruiz	131
Drama Momma – Rob Ruiz	132
Quote – Emily Navarro	133
Home – Rob Ruiz	134
Quote – Rob Ruiz	135
Quote – Rob Ruiz	136
A Third Part of Me – Emily Navarro	137, 138
Quote – Rob Ruiz	139
"D" Batteries – Emily Navarro	140, 141
What's it like – Emily Navarro	142
Outro – Rob Ruiz	143
Outro – Emily Navarro	144
Curtain Call	145

she loves me

Love

Amor

Amour

Amore

Liebe

Liefde

Förälskelse

влюбленность

αγάπη

حالة حبّ

he loves me not

Forgive Me

In the midst of the storm I arose from my sleep
Searching through the fierce winds for my memories
Not remembering my name or my purpose, I ventured into the unknown
Fearing not the dark, but the fact that I have grown

Piercing visions of a world far away
I wish I could stay and have my enemies pray

Trumpets and flags rage with full glory and might
As I make my way through the masses, legions, multitude, I'll put up a fight

Powerful blows crush my bones and my flesh
I gasp for air as I am overwhelmed by the fresh, death that's upon me now
but I will not bow, as I look to the heavens he will show me how

I will take a stand against evil and hate
I know the hanging black man from the tree can relate
It's too late to contemplate your barren forgiveness on an empty plate

And as for my soul if you kill my body, my shell
My spirit is free
But your regret will be for you to tell

she loves me

What Am I Looking for?

Flying without wings

Navigating through life without a compass

Walking without a path to follow

Dreaming, while unable to sleep

Lost in a world of my own realities

Lost in the emptiness of my room

Lost in the notion of not knowing

Lost in an unfamiliar me

The giant webs of mist in the sky, in unimaginable and infinite shapes, are filled to capacity. Filled with the tears that have changed direction – flowing from my eyes – upwards to the sky

My cheeks have marked roads; trenched by many years, many tears, many dreams, many fears

A reminder, a compilation, a tattoo of my life… marked forever on my face – without shame – without grief – without regrets

So, I stand at a crossroad of multiple choices. Do I follow you?

Do I follow them? Do I take a rest? Do I keep on going? Do I stay content?

I allow all that happens to me that has happened to me… that will happen to me

So I follow no one… I'll lead myself

he loves me not

Gone

My head resting on a pillow of tears
The room is dark
shadows are what cover me tonight
slim sections of light zigzagging over me

Asking myself, "Why the tears?"
"What is it that you're so damned scared of?"

I look around… but no one is home
I sit still and carefully listen
But the silence is too loud
I try to focus… but the darkness is too bright
I'm drowning

I lay back and stare at an empty dark ceiling
and the figure of you presents itself

Why am I not smiling as I normally do when I see you?
I can't see a reason for feeling so alone

Then it dawned on me
you were not walking with me
you were not walking towards me

You were just walking away

No good-bye
no reason why

Gone

she loves me

The Impossible

Came into my life like a cosmic flash
left even faster like Jay-Z and Damon Dash

smiled at me once and my heart was yours
ahhhhhh I feel it now that's the love that pours

once in a lifetime once in a twinkling of an eye
it's no surprise I'm enticed I can finally breathe I laugh and sigh

I'm living now I'm illuminating with the radiant glow of joy
amor es para siempre como mi bandera Boricua yo soy

raging flags and trumpets in the grand parade
I've found my queen in which I enchant with a serenade

I turn to look at an ominous dark cloud
like a mighty king enshrouded with vengeance I fall to my knees
and scream aloud

I turned only for a second a split second even
the world breaks in half as this mighty icon is engulfed with
screaming

the visions pierce my soul
crack through the core of my spirit man the abyss opens up and it's
an endless low

how could you ask me to bury my queen?
HOW COULD YOU ASK ME TO BURY MY QUEEN?
when all that I know is to feel serene
my heart snaps in half my flesh turns to denim jean

I'm cold stiff lifeless without you
this mighty knight will sleep the deep sleep
and awaken at the time that the angels do

he loves me not

Tears of a Clown

On the outside I put on a show for the world to see
smile big and bright and sing happily with glee
On the inside the clay is dry and cracked invisible man that's me

Put forth an astonishing effort of courage and bravery
only to be sold into eternal hell fire slavery

On the outside I put on a great show for all to admire in awe
I jack my jaw shake the hands and smile really pretty for the camera
that's me
On the inside the lights are dimming and signaling the last act
that any of you
will ever see

Engrossed myself and my energy till the end for a friend and a lover
I tell you
this love was but for a fool and the flat line that I feel is nothing
new

On the outside I put on a grand beautiful show for the world to see
on the inside I'm dying always crying
never sighing or taking the time to breathe and relax
my time here is numbered and dwindling
I've pushed my strength and will power to the max

she loves me

El amor

El amor es el sentimiento más perfecto que dios ha creado

Esta en el sol que nos cobija en un solo abrazo

Esta en las estrellas del anochecer que alumbra los caminos para uno no perderse

El amor esta en cada flor que alfombra nuestro planeta tierra, acordandonos que con el amor, siempre existe la belleza

El amor esta en la espuma del mar, que limpia y cobija la arena y las rocas, sin pensar en cual vale más la pena

El amor esta imprimido en todo creado e inspirado por Dios

La unión de dos seres llenos del amor, puro y verdadero, siempre es bendecida

he loves me not

Without Saying Goodbye

It was a crisp clear night. I smiled as the breeze enchanted my senses. You held my hand tight and reassured me that I was safe. I was young at heart and free spirited. The moon smiled back as we walked past the park, a friendly wooden bench greeted us and invited us to sit, and we sat and talked for what seemed like three lifetimes. The night was quiet and it was safe and still. I could hear the sound of freedom pump through my veins, I felt euphoric and connected to nature, connected to you. I was swept away by my surroundings and didn't notice how long it had been, that you stopped holding my hand and talking about the midnight sky with me. I cried for help but there was no answer, we were too far into the wooded area for anyone to hear me. I pounded on your chest and I pounded on the ground, but you wouldn't wake up to continue our lovely walk. I stood on my feet and with all my fury and might I loudly beckoned for the hands of time to freeze and to not be so unforgiving. That mighty answer was NO. It was silent, too late, too little, your face grew cold, your strength left your body, and I was left with a memory, the memory of our last walk through the crisp clear night.

she loves me

2007

I'm feeling nauseated. Been in bed all damn day, not wanting to move, not wanting to eat, and not wanting to even breathe.

I'm in my large room, and as big as it is, I feel cramped up in a corner and walls closing in on me… ceiling pushing itself down over my head like an anvil… heavy anvil being pressed on me by some unknown force.

Looking back, I feel sick to my stomach. Feeling that a whole year has passed right before my eyes. And what do I have to show for it?

Did I not try hard enough?

Did I just not care?

Where was I, while the world continued on its natural course?

Where was I, while I was trying to find ME?

I feel lost. Like one of the millions of rain drops that fall from the sky. Unnoticeable… uniquely the same as all the others…hurdling from the darkest of clouds… just to be splattered against the cold dark pavement.

Is there a possibility?

Is there a way out of such despair?

And the problem seems to be that I actually do know that there is. I have a heart full of faith and hope, but my mind, being full of worries and confusion, tends to outweigh the heart at times.

As the count-down begins for the New Year…

he loves me not

I will count the blessings I received and took for granted till the realization of the end of the year… and as the New Year rings in… I will be in deep thought… praying, meditating and filling myself with positive energy, this way I will not have to repeat what I just wrote.

she loves me

Why Have You Forsaken Me?

I prayed for many seasons for many people and for many reasons

and now that I need the blessing
is there no one on their knees confessing?

that I've been good and loyal, till the end like a royal?

reached out to those that felt betrayed
reached out to those that went astray
now give me the comfort as I did for you this very day

your hands don't reach me Lord
your silence and distance is slashing me like the ancient Samurai sword

I believed in you when they pinned you to that tree
I even said God forgive me for I have sinned against thee

so where are you now that I need you the most?
your presence I can't feel it's become a ghost

they may say this is blasphemy and that may be so
if I can't go to the Father, then where the hell else do I go?

Again I Cry

I awaken from a beautiful dream and reality sinks in
So I cry
I look to see that you are not here and reality sinks in
So I cry
I check to make sure my two angels are tucked away in bed and reality sinks in
So I cry
Four beautiful glossy brown eyes that ask so much yet so little of me and reality sinks in
So I cry
Cleaning a home or rather, just a house and reality sinks in
So I cry
Sitting alone, no phones ringing, no knocks at the door, no sound, just candle light
Reality sunk in… again, I cry

she loves me

Flash Love

It was the month of a million beautiful promises
I knew that you loved me and your desires became my very wishes

We walked in bliss couldn't miss the energy from your soul
touched my cheek and my lips so that I would know

We grew so I knew what to do next
I wasn't perplexed I was hexed and eventually vexed
by your actions and reactions what happened to all the love from above?
as quickly as this poem ended, the love was sent off
with a bright white dove

he loves me not

Despierta

Palabras bonitas,
Pero del corazón, nada

Como una sombra
siempre tiene una historia que contar
pero quedas en silencio

Pintastes castillos en mi cielo
estrellas brillaban como diamantes

Lo que pense ser mi realidad, solo resulto ser una fantasia

Me sentia multi-millonaria, después descubrí que fue un cheque en
blanco que intente cobrar en un banco de ilusiones
Tus cuentas eran falsas y los fondos nunca existian

Contigo aprendí, por un breve instante
volar sobre los arco-iris, correr sobre el agua, viajar a diferentes
mundos y montar estrellas fugaz

Despues, el sol ceso de brillar
Mi cielo se torno gris
los relámpagos explotaron
golpes dañinos
dolores inmensos y profundos

Al instante reaccione
y llore sobre mi almohada
Me di cuenta que no fue un sueño
Pretendiste querer mi corazon, y después lo abandonaste

she loves me

Paradise Lost

Mi vida es una nube negra
one that whispers in the breeze, mist of invisible tears
hovering over an island, far, far away
la noche no perdonas, ni me recuerdas
as it launches me onto the glass sidewalks that shatter
along with my corazon
wishing I felt the peace of my sweet Bohios
Los Bohíos también te amo
you cradled me when I was lost, fuerza en mi tribulación
faith to smile again
pero aqui no ay descanso
my legs restless against the pavement they smack on
as a drunkard that has stumbled away from the path
forgive me Lord for I have greatly sinned
I have loved your creation more than you
y conozco que la nube negra fue por desobediencia
and bitter resentment
Islita porque no me salvas como me salvaste en el año de muerte
bring me the comfort I once felt
as the painter smiles at his mighty strokes
a portrait of an eternal paradise, one that I will never leave
engrave my soul on the canvas
so that I may have a permanent home
and not have to relive this nightmarish hurricane
away from the peaceful shore

Reflection

I've said goodbye to love so many times
I've closed the doors, added dead bolts
I've propped chairs to protect myself
I've shut the windows, drawn the curtains and sealed the shutters
I cut my heart out
I bound my hands, and blinded my eyes
Not long after, I found myself in the dark and alone
Longing for the same love that put me in the darkened room of my soul
Not everything you want, is everything you need

she loves me

*Dedicated to my father
Juan Bautista Navarro 07/27/26 - 08/06/2006
...but lives on forever*

Daddy's Little Girl

She had a shoulder to cry on
She had a lap to nap on
She had security that all would be well
She had a love that was stronger than heaven and hell
She had reality in front of her eyes
She had strength to continue on
She had knowledge of years past her own
She had a friend that never left her alone
She had his hands to hold on to hers
She had his arms to keep her warm
She had his words that made everything better
She had his prayers that followed her wherever
And now he's gone
And she still carries with her
the love of her father
that blesses her through every endeavor
Daddy's little girl
forced to live life without her hero
knows that though he physically isn't with her
like a shadow, his spirit will never leave her

he loves me not

I Watch While I Wait

A tear runs down my cheek in the thought of where you are
In the knowing you are creating peace
My tears are of love, fear and hope
Praying one day, you'll find your way back home
And my tears will create a river and will flow to the oceans and seas

And a path will be created so that you can return to me
At night when you are sleeping, I'll be watching over you
My thoughts and prayers will create a dream
Only to be shared by you and I

The day will come when you leave this place and join me up above
A bond unbreakable by life or death… the truest form of love

she loves me

"great sex makes you love bad people"

Repented Heart

The Furious one with a gun not looking back on the run
exploding symphonies of regret on my mind and it weighs a ton

Unrelenting vengeance in my heart for those that betrayed
neglecting the God of salvation to whom I once prayed

Delivering pain in packages of unforgiving hands
not wanting to fall back but rather take a stand
against my own destruction the breaking of a Holy man
Lord forgive my indifference forgive my unrepentance
for the things that I've done with great Fury and undeniable malice

The seasons have changed and arranged my soul in parts
the new season will come and help me to construct a new heart
break the foundations of my anger and let's go back to the start

she loves me

Love Lost

How do I show love when love doesn't show me how?
twisted in memories of good times and laughs
hurtful to the thought and painful to the touch
piercing visions of a new life, frightful at best
and to the rest I say this knight has been exposed to the day
to be left to pay for the mistakes of many
but an army will rise in defense of my death
in triumphant savagery for the discrowning of a just ruler
rise from the dust mighty legion and forsake the wicked
as my red oracle is frozen in time

he loves me not

Carry It With You

Life is so precious... painful at times, scary, and even doubtful...but it is precious. If we abuse it, we lose it. If we take care of it, it takes care of us. If we embrace it, we go the max. We never know for how long this precious gift is going to last us. We don't know how long our loved ones will be around us. So as long as u can love...love with everything you have, as long as you can share, share with the whole world. And as long as you can say I love you, never be ashamed to say it aloud. I love you and always will… for the body is just flesh and bones… the love is carried with us forever.

she loves me

It's Over

No more lies

No more tears

No more arguments

No more uncertainties

No more hiding

No more playing games

No more questioning of honor and loyalty

No more feeling insecure

No more thoughts of "what if"

That's it… it's over

I want to spend my whole life with you

I'm ready

I love you

he loves me not

The Journey

A new chapter to capture and rapture me to a new level
lying devil how you cursed me so
lying devil how you made me to not know
the demise in your eyes the destruction of your lies
and here I am lonely and cold not trying to be bold
just calling to be told that I was once the breaking of a mold
but hear me now for I am faithful and true
my loyalty betrayed and I just don't have a clue what to do
but I'll be strong like before so bring on what's in store
I fear not what's behind this new rusty door

she loves me

Looking for Love

In the deepest of deeps neglecting my sleep
so that I may reap the longing in my soul for an angel of mercy
I see through the blurred promises and walk upon the boiling rivers
to wrap myself in warmth and heal my dreams of endless shivers
This journey has scorched my feet beyond comfort
not giving me rest and dulling the zest
that I once had for fantasies and messages in bottles
that I threw into the watery abyss to act as my decree
Among palaces and villages I've searched
in vain to slip on the slipper of my desire
on the princess of nations soon to be the Queen of patience
As we walk ever so carefully
into the unknown realm

he loves me not

"love doesn't have a catch"

she loves me

What Am I?

For what I have is a culmination of stars wanting to be wished upon
For what I am is a bouquet of orchids
Delicate, tangible, and very fragile
For what I give is a ray of sunshine in the dark
A crystalline drop of rain in the desert
A helping hand to those in need
A clown to project laughter on a smile unseen

he loves me not

En Dedicación a Mi Amigo
In Dedication of My Friend
Rest in Peace

Vinnie,

    We didn't get the time we always wanted, but we appreciated the time that was given to us. May you feel safe wrapped in the arms of our God and your head finally caressed by your mother, as you always wished for. You will be missed so much my bello Vinnie. I will always keep you in my prayers. There will never be anyone that can duplicate what you meant to me. Voy a extrañar tu voz y tus dulces palabras, tus exitosos consejos y tus regaños siempre llegando a buen tiempo. Eres ahora un brillante ángel paseando por las nubes y velando por aquellos que tú adoras en la tierra. Yo estaré mirando hacia el cielo cada noche, como siempre decíamos, y encontrare un poco de consolación sabiendo que estas mirando la misma luna que yo.

she loves me

"Instead of asking myself, "What's going to make me happy?"…

I've decided to ask myself

"What IS my happiness?"

he loves me not

El Espacio

Una silla se queda sola sin ocupar
Un espacio vació donde antes estabas tu
Por el pasillo, ya no te vemos entrar
Ya esta oscureciendo y no te veo llegar

Te siento a cada momento
Pero aun no te veo
Sigo conversando contigo
Pero a mi lado no estas
No me llega el abrazo que me dabas en las mañanas
Pero a la hora de acostarme y de recitar mi oración, siento tus labios rozar mi frente, tal como lo hacías ayer

Mucho tiempo a pasado
Pero todavía no encuentro la manera de decirte adiós
¿Porque tengo que despedirme de ti, cuando te llevo profundamente en mi ser?

Prefiero vivir tu memoria y esperar nuestra gran reunión
Donde una vez mas, tus brazos sentiré, y ese espacio que un día estaba en blanco, se llenara con la luz de tu ser

she loves me

Imagine

Imagine if you will
The strength of a thousand gorillas
Thrashing against your soul propelled by the sails of rejection
Your breath sucked by whirling vacuums of agony

Imagine if you will
The force of infinite G forces
Pushing forward incinerating your will and your desire
Your spirit imprisoned for a billion generations

Imagine if you will
The magnitude of planet sized quakes
Cracking your spirit imploding your eardrums to the sound
Your mind lost in the abyss of tainted sanity

If you can imagine these things with clarity and understanding
...then you my friend, have loved and lost in your lifetime

Accidental Love

I am as a child in this
Too meek to make a defensive sound
My smile reveals my inexperience
Extending my hand with both eyes closed
Feeling around for a hand to hold on to
Stepping forward with eyes yet tighter
Lunging now, I know you'll catch me
Trust is the foundation
A flawed foundation but nonetheless my foundation with you
You caught me
I was safe
I did however land on top of you
so you had no choice but to catch me
As I said
I am as a child in this

she loves me

Just When I Decided

Just when I decided on giving up
You happen to walk in the room
Your smile brightened up my days
Your eyes bewildered my nights
Your voice filled my heart with peace
Your touch brought me back to life
A tear I shed for those I loved in the past
I don't regret the heartache and I never feel that it was a waste of time
I cherished the thoughts of, what once was, and look forward to loving again
Just when I decided on giving up… you happened to walk in to my life

Touch

Feel
Embrace
Grab
Tug
Pull
Grasp
Hold
Latch
Penetrate
Ejaculate
Feel my embrace
grabbing and tugging
pulling and grasping you
hold on love
latch on to me
as I penetrate and ejaculate
Touch
Repeat

she loves me

"are you prepared to accept love?"

he loves me not

It's Time

Many suns have fallen
They've come and gone
Like a firefly with no glow

The oceans are frozen
Now I can walk on water

Lava pours from the screaming mountain
Engulfing my thoughts
It burns

My heart rips in the presence of your indifference
I was your friend

I've been sold to slavery
Sorrow is my new master

My bones are old and weak
They crack against the pavement

Release me my Queen…

Ungrip your stronghold
Hell hath no fury
It burns, deep beneath my skin
Into my essence it burrows

It's time my Queen
My imprisonment must cease
Tomorrow gets near

That is where he is
Black cloak covering his sickle
It will be revealed
I will be its victim

she loves me

It's time my Queen

Release your potion
Un-hex my heart
On my knees, I beg of you

Growing weary is daily for me
Have I not suffered enough?
    Have I not suffered enough?
        Have I not suffered enough?

My kingdom is in shambles
All the guest's are gone
My servants are asleep, eternally

The moon has no shine
Only laughter

Redeem your friend
The king of honors past

Release me!

Help me!

Time is almost invisible
Save me from the fiery dragon
Slay my pain
Allow not the darkness to comfort me

Let it be your words, let it be your words
Forgive me as I forgave you

For it is time… it's time

Lesson Learned

There is a box we all keep
Full of hopes, wishes, and dreams
Full of happy thoughts, wonderful memories
Sweet surprises, goals accomplished, and fantasies waiting to be fulfilled
Then we open this box, and welcome others into it, so that they too can share these experiences They can add to this beloved box, a bit of them with a bit of you
You expect this box to get bigger, wider, deeper, because there are now two sets of everything Yours, and theirs
In time, the box is almost empty
The dreams you kept in it – poof! You woke up
The wishes - blew away like a candle's light
The hopes and fantasies - like mist in the sky
Sweet surprises became sour notes to a once beautiful song
The goals you had already accomplished - seem no longer to matter
Yet the box is not completely empty
for every wish, every dream, every hope, and fantasy that is no longer in it, tears take their place
The box leaks, therefore you have nothing to show for all your efforts
You shared it with them that did not appreciate it, did not respect it, and did not deserve it
Lesson learned

she loves me

Amor

It is when it rains softly
When leaves reveal their orange
Hovering upon us
Like rays from the sun's abundance
It is when children invoke innocence
When worries are washed away
Tickling our toes
like waters of a far away island
Amor was us
it could be us
it should be us

Finding Him

I miss him... yet, I have never had him

I long for his touch of silk and satin skin... even though he has never held my hand, caressed my cheek, or pressed against my chest

I ache every morning to awaken in his arms... to feel the safety of his breath against the back of my neck, the sound of his moans as he gets cozy spooning my body

I feel a calm desperation consume my very being just at the thought that I'm on his mind... that as the butterflies do their acrobatics in my mid section... they leave and take flight... heading directly to him and subsequently, landing on his air-strip of nerves

I want him...
I yearn for his intelligence to engulf my neurons
to expand my horizons with his every word

I desire him... I fantasize of our meeting... of that one split second that our sight meets in unison... emotions explode... our surroundings infected by our heat. Emotions implode... our very beings overwhelmed by such indescribable pleasures

He is the one...
I've said it many times before...but it's the first time I have started to feel it in my veins... like second nature... the feeling of blood flowing through those very veins from the tip of my toes to the pours on my face...

He runs through me
and once again
I live

she loves me

You Never Knew

It's unfortunate and hurtful to realize that the one you thought you knew... you never knew at all

A man you have given your heart and soul to... Although you were afraid to tell him how you felt, because you wanted to make sure it was the same between the two of you. But the signs were there... you both looked forward to seeing each other again

Your inner most passions, letting yourself feel free with him... feel so safe when you wake up in his arms and willing to start a new day with his smile

Your deepest of secrets... things you were ashamed or scared to tell anyone else... you trusted and confided in him

The man you lived some of your most sensual moments with, where there was a feeling of security to just let go... and let him just melt into your body and become one with him. Where there were no longer limits and seeing each other naked was no longer embarrassing

A man who you wanted so hard to be with, but situations rarely permitted for those moments to come true... you figured, the harder things are to get... the more worth they have

A man you hoped would be the reason you stopped looking for anyone else... because no one ever came close
You never knew at all

You never knew what his agenda was... except, that you are no longer part of that agenda, and was never even told. You had to find out... the same time everyone else did

Because there was no sign... there was no telling
you just never knew at all

he loves me not

"You took away the one thing that made my heart beat…

you"

she loves me

Soar

In suspended animation I await your arrival
my body frozen to degrees beyond prehistoric measurements

My mind still and calm serene and steady
thinking does not exist for thinking clouds clarity

Awaiting an heir to the throne of my essence
a partner of support and strength and softness

Take flight beyond the mountains and seas and ascend to the heavens
the Earth is beneath you now, a speck, a fragile ornament

Incinerate warp speeds so that our hearts may have been together for years
if only time travel existed, the ills of my soul would have been purged

The sonic booms acknowledge that you are near
the clouds departing and making way as to accept your Angelic presence

Your iron device has arrived in my world
we are no longer galaxies apart and the mystery has been solved
there is in fact
life, and love, in other universes

he loves me not

"when you tell someone, I love you

it would be wise to know what it would mean to the other person

rather than just say it because it was cute"

she loves me

"don't dare love anyone else before you've dared to love yourself"

he loves me not

Heartbreak Manifesto

We met
I said hello
You said hi
Went for coffee
Then a show
Then you looked at me with those soft sweet green eyes while the performance was in its third act and I felt afraid to move to talk to whisper to think, you had me
We walked out
You hummed
I listened
You plotted
I took the bait and accepted your smile within the soul of my spirit protected by a mystical God force that I could never call by name for he told me never to call upon him unless my heart was being ripped from me by beastly savages
You giggled
I smirked
You leaned forward
I closed my eyes
You ran from me as fast as you could to get away from what we or I or you so confused were falling for each other although we are or were strangers just enjoying a night at an old coffee house and small theatre company
You slipped
I caught you
You thanked me
I leaned forward again
This time you kissed me so deeply so passionately so intensely so divinely so truthfully I'm captured and smitten and in trouble for you're running again only further and further and further can't reach you

she loves me

You waved goodbye
I just stood there
You smiled
I'm picking up the pieces

he loves me not

Me enamore... de el

enamorada de una foto

de una voz

de una simple ilusión

de una sonrisa que prácticamente podría ver al decirme los buenos días

de unos ojos que sentia brillar cuando le daba las buenas noches

enamorada de una fantasia

de alguien que cerca podría tener

pero cuando mas lo quería, más lejos se desaparecía

enamorada de un sueño

de los detalles que resultaban ser el hombre ideal

un corazon que latía solo por el, ya no late, solo muere en soledad

amando a alguien que no me ama

dolor difícil de explicar

solo guardare los bellos recuerdos

que para el, quedaron en el ayer

me enamore... de el

she loves me

Plegaria

Gigante luna
Que me despiertas con tu luz
Oye mis llantos
Que grito en las noches
Pidiendo un amor
Puro y sincero
Tranquilo sin apuros
Que sea solo mío
Que encuentre en mí
Un tesoro antes desconocido
Que despierte en mí,
Sueños ocultos
Que me haga sentir
Como la única y mejor mujer
Que en su vida me demuestre,
Que soy dichosa de ser su amante

he loves me not

"the love I can bring is based on the love I feel for myself"

she loves me

"you don't understand the price that must be paid for love…

it's why you never pay attention"

"Why do you want to jump to the conclusion that maybe this beautiful woman you have found... is not going to put up with your "baggage"? Sweetheart, she has shown you that she is patient, and obviously very interested in you. Why not let her decide for herself if she can deal with it? If she cares for you, as she sounds like she does and really wants to be with you, she will understand, she will be patient, and she will wait"

she loves me

Listen

It is easy to ignore my cries for you
your ears implode with indifference

So simply you dismiss when I beckon
your eyes gaze away from my presence

Casually brush my summons to the side
your arms crossed in defiant restraint

Ever so quietly

Softly

I'm invisible to you

But my cries rampage against your mighty ship
tossing it's cargo and men into the great unforgiving sea

I beckon with thunder and lightning
your village a pile of matchsticks as it burns to the ground

My summons delivered by the Mighty Hand of God Himself
restraining his full wrath on your sin

Ever so quietly

Softly

He has taught me to make you, invisible to me

Sacred

Eternal are the vows that you don't respect or uphold
Everlasting are the scars left implanted in your soul mate's spirit
Infinite are the excuses your mind manufactures
Abundant are the tears that stain the silk sheets you never sleep on
Overflowing are the prayers on her lips to the heavens above
Unconditional is her devotion to the one that eludes her warmth
Sacred is the decree that you have broken before God
The punishment for your transgression is equal
Equal to the death you have sentenced her heart to

she loves me

Seasons Change

the season has changed
your heart is unsure
my mind is troubled
our thoughts are divided
the season has changed
your soul is lost in tears
my spirit is longing for you
our love will not die
the season has changed
your pain is justified
my desire is to be with you
our future is now
although the season has changed
my passion for you has not
and our love will blend as one

he loves me not

"love in any dose can cure the ills of the world"

she loves me

Invisible

I kissed your forehead as you slept

but you didn't feel it

I whispered, "I love you", in your ear

but you didn't hear it

I met you on the beach in your dream last night

but you don't remember

I held your hand tightly when you got scared

but you ignored it

I yelled out your name today as you boarded the train

but you thought you imagined it

I prayed hard all day that you would be safe at work

but you never knew it

I looked up at the sky and asked the angels to guide your way home

but you never would have guessed it

Do you even know I exist?

Love Holds No Prisoners

Love holds no prisoners

It frees you from life's chains

Love doesn't make you revel in remorse

Manifesting one's deepest heartfelt emotions, for loves sake

is always made to feel content

not regret it's fear and astonishment

Love sings but soft melodies

As cupid pulls on the gentle silk cords of your hearts instrument

Leading you in a midsummer night's dream of delightful fairies and mischief

Glow thy light of blessed angels that doth keep a watchful eye on heaven's gate

Tell my beloved of earth toned mane to bless thy heart for true loves sake

Of cupid's arrow I do bleed

Pain as sweet as a gentle kiss, but fragile as the petals of a rose out of season

I do give my love to thee

Scrolls of the god's words would not enough nearly be

she loves me

But for every sun's rays I see with thyne eyes, as they bathe the earth's dew with warmth

I give myself to thee

he loves me not

"if your lover loves you more than themselves…

you are headed for pain"

she loves me

Black Blood

You are beyond voodoo-ous
I awaken in cold sweats at the sound of your laughter

Only a pure luciferious nature can allow for such deceit
You drink the vile seepage from decomposing corpses

When I made love to you I felt my innocence escape my flesh
The box of Pandora you kept under your bed sealed it infinitely

You washed your face with the blood of a thousand broken dreams
All your past loves ripping through your skin attempting to escape

Not a soul escapes your dungeon of blackness and terror
The spirits that gave up, walk in agony for generations and generations

My dear, you are an abomination, a sentence from a higher court
The abyss is paradise and I wish to abide in it and not mare of you again

These were the words found in a densely wooded area
Carved on an oak tree by you
Warning those that come after
Never to sell your soul to the reaper
In exchange for love

he loves me not

Personal blog entry: DENY ME?! HOW DARE YOU?!

Who the hell do you think you are,
living a lie that has gone so far?
Denying my existence and my past with you
If she really believes you... she's just another fool

You remember me in the way a child remembers Santa Clause
All through the years, that memory is undeniable
I was the one who made you smile
after so many seasons that you lived in denial
I was the one who woke all of your senses, who made you believe...
that in love, there was still room for second chances

I'm that first beat your heart took,
after years of numbness, cold and untruth
It was me you thought of when your heart got off track
In life there may be second chances,
but rarely will the same love take you back

Through the many times you hurt me, empty promises and no-can-dos,
you caused a heart to split in two, but still in silence, I cherished you
For once upon a time, with you I planned on living my days,
and when that dream was over, In my heart you still remained

Over the years life separated us,
even though the bond continued,
you took on other lovers that could never measure up to me
I know this to be a fact, this you maintain to be true

Now you choose to deny my existence
to another who will follow in your quest
Your answers to her questions about who I am,
"Don't worry, she's my cousin", "my sister", or "just another friend"

she loves me

You see, this is where "our" story ends
I am not a whore you once fucked in bed
I am the woman who brought you back to life
of all the other women, I am the one you should have never denied

So how does a person, like myself, react to undeserving pain?
A final favor as a gift to you, I will gladly pay
I will remove my soul, my love, my very essence from your life
Just as you have edited me to others
with your fictional character, your words, your lies

Don't bother looking for me, forget what you ever felt
My very being you chose not to acknowledge
Therefore, in my life you will no longer exist
GOODBYE and FAREWELL

Suicide
a dark humored short story

    The sirens blared through the neighborhood breaking four straight hours of silence, a rarity. Even the thugs that usually hang out in the front stoop were taking the night off.

    The glow of the red engine shot through my window and I attempted to ignore it but curiosity peaked. I slowly made my way to the window.

    The burly men were ramming the front door with what appeared to be a battering ram. I couldn't see that well without my glasses. I'm going in tomorrow morning to finally get a new prescription. Anyway, they rammed and rammed until they were finally in. From my distance I could see the figures running back and forth from room to room. They stopped. I guess they found what they were looking for.

    No action inside that house for about five minutes. I'll make myself a snack and come back in a few minutes. On second thought, I get heartburn every time I eat this late, I'll hold off until the morning.

    Oh wait, what's this? I see them picking someone up from the bedroom floor. It looks like a man from here. Shit, I can't squint hard enough to really tell though. Hmmm that's strange. The only person I ever saw coming out of that apartment was a nice looking woman that kept to herself. You know, I've seen her for the past five years and I never asked her what her name was.

    Damn who's this? Another woman screaming her head off trying to make her way into the apartment. The cops are holding her back. She keeps yelling for Mark. There's no Mark there lady, just that poor woman. It looks like someone died in there. I'm gonna take a closer look.

she loves me

       Good morning Officer.
       Sir stay behind the red tape.
       What happened here?
       Stay behind the red tape!
       Ok, I heard you. What happened?
       The dude killed himself.
       What dude?
The guy that lived there, would you please stand away from the red tape?
       I'm going back upstairs, there's obviously nothing to see here. I wonder what dude he is talking about though. I never saw a man coming out of that apartment and I've been here for years.
       Good morning honey.
       Good morning.
       You heard about what happened next door last night?
       Yeah a cop told me some dude killed himself. I never saw a man come out of that apartment; I wonder who he was talking about.
       What are you talking about, you saw him almost everyday. Mark, the transvestite.
       Transvestite? I thought that was a woman.
       Yeah he left a suicide note. It was published in the paper this morning. He said he was tired of being invisible to the world.
       Damn. He was invisible to me too. I never would have guessed that was a dude.
       I know honey, that's why we're going in today to finally get your fucking prescription fixed.

he loves me not

A Consequence

I can be as fierce as a mythical beast when those I love are threatened
I can be as sweet as the most perfect peach, if it does well to a child
I can be love, hate, wild and sublime
All it takes is a flick of the switch to make you eternally mine

she loves me

"don't be afraid to say yes to the less attractive…

love will reward you greatly"

My Heart Chose You

Of all the men that have crossed my path, you were the one my heart chose
You see, I have been told every story out of every book
Every line from every song imaginable
Every lie ever believed
Still, my heart chose you
You were different from the rest
You came at me with nothing but sincerity
You caressed my thoughts with your intelligence
You embraced my soul with your sensuality
You immersed my heart in the ocean of your passion
Still, my heart chose you
Darling, I found a beautiful friend whom I can confide in... in you
I found the intellectual conversation that stimulated my mind … in you
I found a love that I thought never existed… in you
Still, my heart chose you
When we fall in love, we think with our hearts and forget to comprehend with our minds
Once again, I fell in love with a lie
and yet my heart… chose you

she loves me

"I can't recall what made me cry the most…

the fact that you broke my heart …

or that I truly believed you would never hurt me"

he loves me not

"look in the mirror…

that beautiful person loves you…

oh to be loved by such a beautiful person"

she loves me

Believe In Yourself

There may be days when you get up in the morning and things aren't the way you had hoped they would be... that's when you have to tell yourself that things will get better.

There are times when people disappoint you and let you down, but those are the times when you must remind yourself to trust your own judgment and opinions. Keep your life focused on believing in yourself and all that you are capable of.

There will be challenges to face and changes to make in your life, and it is up to you to accept them.

Constantly keep yourself headed in the right direction. It may not be easy at times, but in those times of struggle you will find a stronger sense of who you are. So when the days come that are filled with frustration and unexpected responsibilities, remember to believe in yourself and all you want your life to be, because the challenges and changes will only help you to find the goals that you know are meant to come true for you. Keep believing in yourself.

he loves me not

"today love will find you…

completely off guard"

she loves me

Seasons May Change... But the Love Stays the Same

The roses of a pedal eventually get brittle and fall

The water from the well with time does dry out

When a tree gets old, it cracks from within and in due time, falls

Nevertheless, the memory lives on

The marks they leave in our lives continue a new life path

Those moments, that drop of water much needed from the well

The roses' aroma that reminded us that someone truly loved us

The shade from the tree that was so necessary will never leave us

It lives on… within us

he loves me not

"love is a bitch"

she loves me

Pillow Talk: As simple as opening your mouth

You never realize how much is said in silence.

How much is "SHOWN" when "IGNORED".

How much is put "IN", when u leave things "OUT".

Things can be misunderstood, misconstrued, misinterpreted, and misrepresented.

Sometimes, things are exactly as you imagined.

When the answer is simple… WHY DON'T YOU JUST SAY IT?!

When you leave a person guessing and wondering, don't blame them if they got it all wrong. They are not mind readers.

…and you had the answers ALL ALONG.

he loves me not

"sex is not love"

she loves me

Distant Desire

The midnight summer air is thick with anticipation
and sleep doesn't find me
I toss and turn and hear the humming of the steel fan at my bedside

It's a calming and soothing effect
which doesn't last long as you engulf my thoughts
I attempt to drift into dreams
and those dreams are interrupted by sudden gasps

I see you gasping in ecstasy over me
as your dark reddish locks tickle my face
Quickly I awaken
my body glistening with perspiration
my muscles tense and pulsating

My window throws me a cool breeze that only seems to enhance what I feel
I close my eyes
The breeze gets cooler and stronger as rain begins to tap against the steamy glass

I walk over to the mist and open my window wider till the wetness of the night drips against my chest
I close my eyes once again as the rain hastens its pace and you appear before me

For miles and miles there are no walls, no trees, no windows, and no civilization
Only two beings locked inside each other breathing simultaneously

Your lips taste the rain against my firmness as the raindrops force you to close your eyes
Your hair is soaked and heavy as I hold on with slippery hands

he loves me not

Your tongue glides and slides on me as you attempt to get a hold of my dripping wet thickness
The rain is deep and strong like your passion

Lightning and thunder forces me to hold you tight as I embrace you from behind
Your breasts heave as I swell inside you while kissing your neck

My name becomes louder and louder as the storm rages into our bodies
You shiver for a moment as you hold my face and release your pressures, and your desires onto me
I wait until a slight decline in your climax as I become engorged and erupt inside you

We are locked in pleasure as the rain trickles down our moist flesh
The breeze enters my room again
my lonely room
where all that is left, is a distant desire

she loves me

"I used to believe that somewhere out there…

my prince will come my way…

I just decided to come *my* way, fuck the prince"

Someday… Just Dosen't Look Like It's Gonna Be Today

Could it be that I am early?

Could it be that I am just too late?

Could it be happening right now, and I just haven't realized it yet?

When will it stop raining in my heart?

Why won't it just mend?

Who is he that has the missing part to this broken heart?

When will it end?

Someday... just doesn't look like it's gonna be today

Somewhere, maybe close, or miles away

Someplace, in the place I once had dreamt

Someone will... come my way

You see, I don't know how much more it can take

My unselfish heart isn't afraid

Though it's been broken in two, battered and bruised, it still holds hopes for finding you

And here I wait...

Someday… just doesn't look like it's gonna be today

she loves me

Somewhere, maybe close, or miles away

Someplace, in the place I once had dreamt

Someone will come my way

I ask myself, repeatedly

Why is it that my heart doesn't want me to give in?

Just when I want to give up, just when I want to shut down,

my heart brings back my faith, and a tomorrow full of hope

Someday... just doesn't look like it's gonna be today

Somewhere, maybe close, or miles away

Someplace, in the place I once had dreamt

Someone will come my way

he loves me not

"fuck love

no wait, I didn't mean it…

you know what, yeah fuck love"

she loves me

Dear Love

Dear love,

I've been through a lot of pain in your name. But I know you were not at fault.

I've seen the good, the evil and the unsure through your eyes. But I don't hold it against you.

I've planned my life around you, making sure you are involved in every occasion, every breath and every emotion, but I'm sure you needed time away; you have others to tend to.

Love, I guess I'm selfish. It's not that I want you all to myself, keep you and lock you away where no one can get to you. No. If that were the case, who would love me? Not that it makes much of a difference what anyone does right now.

I guess what I'm trying to say is, thank you. Thank you for being there when you felt you needed to be there and not when I said you need to be there. Thank you for being sincere with me, never hiding the fact that you cautioned me about the pain I would possibly find myself in. For the times I cried my heart out, every tear in your name.

I'm thankful for the smiles you placed not only on my face, but my heart and my soul. For the experiences, those minute moments of happiness I was gifted to have, for the memories of lovers gone by. Thank you for seeing that I am worthy of your efforts, for teaching me that you are something to learn about, learn from, and pass it forward.

Love, thank you for loving me enough to allow me to feel your strengths, weaknesses, hatred and envy. Thank you for loving me as I love you.

he loves me not

For as I always say,

I'm in love… with the idea of falling in love. I look forward to your response.

Love,
Me

she loves me

"rejection opens new doors"

Sparkle

What happened to the sparkle in my eyes?
It was there yesterday and for months before
I remember the first time people noticed it and made me aware it existed
It was the day I met you
Our first words… echoed only by the wind. The feeling in me, which only with fairy dust could it be duplicated, when you first held my hand. Your sweet smile burned in me. The taste of your lips that can only be compared to the softness of a teardrop rolling over one's lips and the taste... sweeter than the word "love" itself
As time passed, that sparkle in my eye grew brighter. My smile exhumed the truest happiness ever felt. My laughter was to be envied and my emotions, instead of a roller coaster, became a beautiful merry-go-round of magical glistening unicorns and mermaids
Then, yesterday came… and my sparkle dimmed
My smile was now on "MISSING" posters
My heart was nowhere to be found
My life, as a whole, had meaning... but no profound sense of being

she loves me

"love is not to be understood, just accepted"

he loves me not

Pillow Talk: End of a chapter

I see that a certain chapter of my life has now come to a close. What at one time made me smile, only brings out remorse.

I wrote and wrote about the laughs and the tears, which once upon a time, filled my days with much joy and less fear.

For you see, life is just a rough draft, as I unfortunately have come to learn. Sometimes we must tear out those chapters that are no longer functional or useful in the story of lessons learned.

Scratch out a word here, correct the spelling there, replace the names of useless characters with those who really care.

I've learned that to complete my story… I have to weed out what pains me… I have to delete that which was in my way. I have to erase the illusions that once fooled my eyes and whiteout the emotions that betrayed me.

I have allowed myself to be sidetracked, to be fooled and taken advantage of, but this is where it ends.

There will no longer be a need for footnotes at the bottom of my pages to explain the who, what, why, where, how and when… It will, as it has always been, be written in black and white, on paper, with pen.

It was nice knowing you, and I wish you the best. But now I see that to complete my happy ending… you were never to exist.

she loves me

Eternal

The storms and dreams engulf my memory
of a time less forgiving, of a time less adoring
Fierce blows to the growth, binding my free will
Not enduring I seek shelter as I did as a child
Feeling the comfort of a present heaven
I wish not to escape and venture, into the unknown
Like a lamb to the slaughter I stand the accused
My thoughts and *rememberings* betray me
Tormented by dejavu, I'm here to stay, oh only if you knew
My honor in tact, my pride thrown about
The mighty truth will prevail and be my redeemer in the midst of your doubt
Latching on to a beacon of light and illuminating your sight
Transgressions of the flesh, failings of the heart, are not for this knight
The day will reveal my soul; I have not a thing to hide
I have but a thing to share
My love for all eternity
And eternity for all my love

he loves me not

"when claiming to be "not like all the others"…

do it while facing your reflection…

you just may find out you were lying to yourself all along"

she loves me

In Search of

but have you ever found love from above
flowing to the surface like distant doves
when it hurts so badly and you're glad
that the abyss has made you go stark raving mad
I've felt the burn and learned
that it was all but a mere dream so it seemed
as it cleaned out my soul and I lost control
have you ever found love or anything for that matter?
I'm still searching and learning and holding on to the pieces
before they turn to dust and scatter

he loves me not

The Star to the Left of the Moon

I'll be there for you when you need my love. When you need someone, I will not move
I will never leave you and though the sky is full of light, that's the time I'm sending you my blessings within the sky
When the sun has fallen to rest and the night has darkened the sky
I am the star to the left of the moon... I will be your guide
Call on me, let me feel your pain. Call on me, let me hear your cries. Call on me when your heart is full of you... Call on me when you just can't understand
In these times of pure uncertainty, one thing remains to be true
When you need me, I'll be right there
The star to the left of the moon

she loves me

The Core

In the heart of every man lives a beast
an untamed phenomenon that can devour a nation
and bring furious war to the world
A being so fierce that the earth trembles at the very mention of its name
In my heart there lived such a creature
he dwelled within me and through me
A sonic boom penetrated the core and unholy warfare preceded
among the entanglement and barbaric blows there I stood
In silent chaos
The victor
for all to see in heaven and hell
the beast no longer abides in me
He has been slain
by the mighty power of love

Myths

Tears are meant to fall

Hearts are meant to break

Love is meant to hurt

These are all lies we set ourselves up for

It's up to us to diminish the myths and bring out the truth

she loves me

Elisa's Garden

Your hair as Daisies lips as roses
not withholding the sun's rays and majestic doses
Tulip eyes and fresh breeze whispers
you enchant me at the midnight hour
If only for a moment water my spirit with your rivers of salvation
If only for a moment shower my soul with the soft moon
If I can walk in the midst of the storm hand in hand
I can and shall walk in the midst of the storm flesh to flesh
Summer Spring Winter and Autumn gathers my strength and I surrender
I surrender to your colors and love and beauty and essence
Carnation scent from your soft sweet face
and now I know that I am in heaven, in the Kingdom, the Angel's palace
Thank you for allowing me a moment in your stellar presence
A growth of desire a hope for brightness and clarity
In the Garden of your strength I shall be set free, free for all eternity
to embed the roots into my veins
and embed your love into my soul

he loves me not

2 Seconds Until Forever
a dark humored short story

Peter felt the barrel of the pistol pressed against his left temple. His eyes wrinkled shut as a droplet of moisture raced down his chubby red cheek. He clinched his right fist, maybe to absorb whatever impact came from a blast. It was only fitting that it all end like this. After all, the rest of the week was also shitty.

Monday started like any other Monday for the insurance broker. The metal alarm clock blared and echoed through the one bedroom apartment like a lonely ferryboat horn along a foggy river. Slowly he came to his feet after a long hearty stretch that cracked a bone or two. The bathroom was only about 20 feet away but seemed like 20 blocks through hazy, tired, sad eyes. As he dragged himself to the bathroom sink, he could still hear the sound of last night's door slamming, after another meaningless romp with the visitor from Germany that moved next door. Ten minutes was about the average time that Peter spent in the bathroom, and that included brushing his teeth, shaving, getting rid of last night's cold pizza, and a birdbath.

The closet somehow became the storage room and clothes were conveniently flung on top of the treadmill. Peter liked dark colors. Brown is always good for Mondays he thought. Nothing exciting ever happens on the first day of the week anyway, at least not at the office. There was no need of ironing the brown polyester suit since no one ever saw him at work. All the transactions were done by phone. Shaving wasn't really a necessity either but he would cut himself purposely sometimes. He liked the pain and the slight sight of blood slowly appearing on his chin. Sometimes he wished he had the guts to cut himself deeper but hoped things could and would change. Maybe that's why he kept a photo of his ex-wife on his worn nightstand, even while rolling in bed with the hefty German.

she loves me

Breakfast was in the fridge and ready to eat. There was still a slice of pizza and about a half can of beer. Peter somewhat got his appetite back after his youngest son began to call him dad again. Hearing his son refer to him by his first name hurt him almost as much as his wife receiving full custody last year.

The phone rang just before Peter headed out the door. "Hello," he said almost surprised since his phone hasn't rung in about 2 months. He was quite surprised and startled by the unfamiliar sound. "But how could that be?" He gave an awkward gasp as he fell to his knees and began to cry like the baby his ex-wife says he is. To this day it's unclear who made the call, but at any rate, it was a reliable and credible source. Just one year after receiving custody of her three children, Peter's ex-wife decided to take her children's lives and then her own. He didn't think much of the letters he was getting from her regarding her depression and addiction to sex with strange men. Sex with any man except him was satisfying to her.

Peter always blamed his dismal marriage to periodic bouts of sexual deficiency. It didn't help that he was shot in the groin during the Gulf War, by friendly fire.

If only he'd have taken those letters seriously he'd at least have his children, at least have his delusions of reigniting an unhealthy relationship with a woman that loved to scratch his face because she liked the way he shrieked while making love to her.

His sobbing went on all night. He didn't even move from the spot he plopped down on. It never occurred to him to jump on the bus and go uptown to see what the hell was going on. He figured, why torture himself. There was also a twisted sense of relief that his ex wife couldn't be with the kids either.

Two days passed and Peter was a visual mess of a man, if one even dares to call him a man. Bags accompanied his sleep deprived eyes. He'd always had them, they were just amplified now.

he loves me not

He slowly picked up the ringing phone wishing that what he heard from the very reliable and credible source was somehow a joke, a mistake. No words from the source, just his best friend Stephen, finally reaching him after two days of banging on his door.

"Hello," Stephen said loudly, since Peter didn't say a word.

"Stephen?"

"Yes it's me Peter. How are you? Are you alright?"

"They're dead."

"I know. Look, everybody's worried sick about you. It's been a couple of days since anyone has seen you. Pull yourself together and come to my house. Better yet, I'll pick you up."

"No Stephen, no. They're dead."

"Peter, you have to come out of your house and make arrangements for your family." Peter began to cry to himself as he heard those words. He covered his mouth with his hand as if Stephen couldn't hear him already. He slammed the phone down and began to cry out loud.

There was a loud bang at the door. Peter managed to drag his corpse to the peephole. Two neatly pressed police officers were at his door. The good cop said, "Mr. Sullivan, It's the police. Please open the door. We'd like to chat with you. Make sure you're okay in there." Peter held his finger over the peephole. Maybe they'll see him. The bad cop gave him about a good twenty seconds and began to bang on the door loudly. "Sullivan! You open this goddamn door now! I can see your shadow under the door!" He couldn't see a darn thing. Just bluffing like a veteran cop only knows how to do. And with that, Peter opened the door. "Mr. Sullivan," began the good cop, "we were called by a friend of yours. He was concerned for you. We were informed of the tragedy and we're really sorry." The bad cop stretched his arm towards Peter's chest and at the end of his fingertips was a blue and white 1-800- hotline card. "Call this number if you need help with anything, twenty-four hours a day. Let's go John." The neatly pressed officers put on their crisp hats and headed out the door. The rookie cop looked back and shook his head.

she loves me

Peter closed the door and ripped the card into little pieces. He staggered to his bed and his weakened body disappeared into the flat pillows.

He rose up about two and a half days later. His bed was a bit wet from night sweats and spilling cheap wine. He actually managed to ignore the fact that he should've sought out his family and prepared proper burial procedures.

In his mind, his ex-mother-in-law would control the arrangements, just as she controlled their wedding. He knew he would never see them again so what difference did it make. The vile woman hated him more than she hated her daily bouts with painful constipation.

Peter had lost his wife, his children, his job, and his purpose. He thought, "I should end it now."

Then there was a familiar bang at the door. This time he didn't drag himself. He already hatched a plan to take care of his misery. In his nightstand he had a .22 caliber pistol that he bought after he was mugged about six months ago. The sooner he could get rid of whoever the hell was tormenting him at the door, the sooner he could get rid of his agonizing misery.

His peephole was engulfed with a hugeness that he could recognize from the top of a skyscraper. He figured; why not go out with a bang. So he opened the door to his obese German neighbor and quickly hurried her inside.

She didn't have a television set, so there was no way she would be able to connect the face on the screen to the face of the recently deceased sitting on top of Peter's nightstand. The murder-suicide had been on the news all week. She didn't speak or understand English either, so there was no way she could hear about the ordeal down at the local beauty salon, not that she ever went there anyway. All she understood was a groping hand on her enormous tank of an ass and the tugging of her 42DD bra, which Peter had no trouble removing just seconds after she entered the door.

he loves me not

He led her to the bedroom like a farmer leading his cows to green pastures. Peter pounced on her and fantasized about being a cowboy in a rodeo. She just kept saying, "Jes, jes, jes." He found it a bit odd that she almost made sense, "Did she just say yes?" he thought, but he quickly dismissed it and gave her four ridiculously powerful thrusts. She melted in ecstasy and he turned his head to the photo of his now permanent ex-wife, as if to let her know what she could've had if she'd only taken him back and not shot herself to death. That pathetic moment of victory quickly passed as he was overcome with emotion and began to cry like a howling fool.

Glenda was emotionally crushed at his obvious plea to his ex of, "Oh please love me, as I love you," and shoved him off her sweaty pale flesh. He didn't even try to break his fall and landed awkwardly against the wall. Still wailing like a baby.

Peter had showed off his gun to Glenda, even though she didn't understand what the hell he was saying, about two months prior. Bad for him, good for her.

She only wanted to scare him a little. Just to show him how much she really cared. To show him that his indifference to her efforts, like enrolling in night class at the local college and learning how to say yes, or jes, or whatever English they're teaching. Or how she let him have his little photo on his nightstand as long as she could come over after a hearty meal and have sex with him. She was already in love with this frail, empty, shell of a man, but he didn't know it. And now he has handed her the ultimate betrayal, crying for another woman while practically making her cry in bed, at the same time.

And so she lunged. Well, it was more like she moved, toward the gun in the nightstand drawer. She only wanted to scare him a little. He didn't even notice the barrel moving closer to his head. His tears were blurring his vision. He didn't need to see to know that the barrel of his .22 caliber anti-mugger was now pressed against his temple. He quickly stopped his sniveling.

"Glenda love ju!" I guess night school was paying dividends. "Glenda ju hurt! Why ju no love Glenda?"

she loves me

Peter just sat there dumbfounded. He didn't answer. Maybe her accent threw him off. Whatever the case, his eyes wrinkled shut as a droplet of moisture raced down his chubby red cheek. He clinched his right fist, maybe to absorb whatever impact came from a blast. It was only fitting that it all end like this.

She only wanted to scare him, but his unfortunate indifference made her rage. She yelled something in German and pulled the trigger. She pulled again and again. Three pulls and not a single shot rang out. No bullets in the gun. She quickly came out of whatever trance she was in and threw the gun across the room. Then she ran out the door. Well, it was more like, she moved out the door.

Peter finally opened his cowardly eyes. He looked around for his burly assailant but she was gone. All that was left was his empty existence and a sudden recollection to his gun's inability to fire a single shot.

About five months ago his ex-wife asked him for help in purchasing a gun. She knew he had one for protection and figured she needed one too. She wanted protection from him. If he knew she had a gun maybe he would layoff the phone calls for a long time and not suddenly pop up wherever she was. He declined her request to purchase a gun and wondered why she even needed one. He later agreed to give her some ammo for a .22, in which he said would be a perfect gun for her to conceal in her purse. He didn't think she would actually get one.

So he met her at the park, with ammo in hand. He thought he had am extra box but he didn't. So he went ahead and unloaded ammo from his gun. He figured he would replace it later. Lucky for him he never did.

Peter sat there and laughed deliriously at his recollection. He cried a little too, okay alot. Not for his ex-wife, he realized she was a selfish monster, but for his children. He did love them after all. He also suddenly thought about Glenda. She could help him through this. She's a strong German woman. Hearty meals and even heartier sex will comfort him he thought.

he loves me not

Peter picked himself up and put his gun away, far away, in the trash. He went next door and knocked on Glenda's door. He could hear a faint, "Who iz et?"

Peter smiled. "It's me, Peter."

Glenda ran to the door. No, she didn't move to the door, I mean she RAN to the door.

she loves me

Tired

Tired of looking and finding nothing

Tired of watching life pass me by

Tired of seeing in black and white through rose colored glasses

Tired of thinking, my head is about to bust

Tired of dreaming, I'd rather never sleep

Tired of hoping, my heart can't compete

Tired of wishing the day will finally come

Tired of crying from sunset till dawn

Tired of talking, my words go unheard

Tired of praying, unanswered go my hopes

Tired of whispering my feelings to the stars

Tired of smiling, pretending what I am not

Tired of laughing, being everyone's clown

Tired of running, just to find myself going around and around

I'M JUST TIRED OF BEING TIRED

Incredible You

Did I think it would happen in a million years after my fears and tears?
not in a billion but resurrected is my hope because you are near

My veins pump the fury of the past
an incarnation of hatred that you'll help me to cast
into the vast open sea
I can see
that you are for me and me for you and I will never falter and flee

My heart beats a trillion symphonies instantaneously with one look
of your cosmic stare

Would the wicked dare to share their poison
because I'm the chosen and your dreams are no longer frozen?

I make a wish a simple decree
that when you think of me
you turn to the sun and know that you and I just became free

she loves me

"hatred of love is hatred of God"

Wrong Number

I picked up the phone to call someone else…
and automatically dialed your number by mistake

But now that I have you on the line... there's something I want to tell you

THANK YOU – For always being there
I'M SORRY – If I ever made you share a tear
I NEED YOU – For you are my pillar of strength
I LOVE YOU – Because you called me by mistake

I meant to tell you... I NO LONGER WANT YOU IN MY LIFE
THAT I AM DISGUSTED EVERYTIME I SEE YOU
I WANTED TO TELL YOU HOW STUPID YOU ARE FOR LETTING EVERYONE WALK ALL OVER YOU

The whole idea of calling you was to tell you how much I HATE YOU

But as soon as I heard your voice, an overwhelming sensation came over me
and I felt the need to tell you

I'M PROUD OF YOU – For trying so hard to make things work for your family

I ADMIRE YOU – For giving your heart to all… even though it's not loved in return

I'VE MISSED YOU – Since you went into hiding because of what others thought of you

she loves me

YOU INSPIRE ME – To continue dreaming my dreams
to reach for every star that I feel I can grasp

I LOVE YOU... Because you are whom I love

I'm glad I called you in error
Who knows what would have happened to me had I not called you
or what would have happened to you had you not called me

I know that I have taken a lot of your time
however, I felt the need to speak and be heard
I know that I have always had a special friend on the other line
funny… it was ME all this time

* I was going through a very painful time in my life, and needed someone to talk to. In the confusion of trying to decide what friend to call, I suddenly heard my voice mail message on the other line. I had dialed my own number and didn't even notice…and in turn, I found a true friend... ME*

Find Myself

Across a path of abandoned dreams
Through the streets of sorrow and avenues of despair
I found myself
Found myself to be lost
Ever increasing pain and yearning for the sun to set
Release me of my soaring roar against my own heart
Engulf my spirit with truth not logic
So that my burning eyes may see her upon the horizon
Release me of my soaring roar against my own mind
Bring upon the love of my longing, my yearning
So that I may find myself amongst the rest of the lost
So that I may find myself
before I find my Queen

she loves me

I Drink to My Heart

You can only tell someone you love them so many times

that doesn't care to hear it - before you start to hear your own echo

You can only show someone how much they mean to you

before your forget yourself in the process

You can only give so much of your heart to someone

who doesn't want it - before you hurt so much, you want to die

As painful as it may be, the way you can really show him you love him so damn much

is to wish him love and say goodbye

Someday, he might actually realize all the things you were to him

but didn't realize it at the time

Maybe not

I drink to my heart that bleeds the excess of you

he loves me not

"your life revolves around loving relationships with people…

disastrous ones too"

she loves me

Death of My Heart

Silently, softly... I lay my sweet love to rest

Cradling her ever so softly… my arms denying their forces to let go

Reflections of a time of wonder and beauty
soon in her eyes would not show

Why damn the killer, why fill myself with hate?

For the only murderous act was giving in to heartache

What futile mission have I set up for myself?
To believe in a world where love has been lost

I bury you now with my deepest regrets… My heart... My soul

May you forever rest

he loves me not

"love yourself more than you actually deserve"

she loves me

You Took

My love you took without hesitation
My hand you promised to have and to hold
My life you sent into a roller coaster ride
Spinning way out of control
My eyes you deceived, my heart you stole
My words you took for granted
However, one thing you could never take away from me
You could never take away my dignity

he loves me not

The Hopeful

The midnight hour has struck with great power and might
my body is weak and my strength is as the blind man's sight

Echoes in my mind of her voice, her sweet violet voice

Imagine the piercing visions of laughter and pain and living and dying

In my heart there's a door, a storage of love
to be opened by the breeze on the wings of doves

Creating and contemplating my next move
but I can't crawl can't walk can't run I'm stuck
can't move I've run out of time and luck

My feet implanted in the quicksand of time

Deliver me and let me know that I will be as the mind in the wind
take me across the waters as I falter
carry my form my spirit and be my safety
I'll never let go of the hope to find love to find peace of mind for all times
just like the beautiful sound of those summertime chimes

she loves me

The Intimate Stranger

In a name rests a mystery of a family history entwined with love and affection
Although the namesake might have been accidental there is no denying the connection
A mother and daughter the mightiest of foundations
A father so proud and strong bursting with anticipation

The glory of the family bond shines through her bold black mane
Aida being Nancie vice versa, yes they are one in the same

Strong Taino features enchanting to the sight and sense
Increasingly divine oh how I wish I can absorb her scent

My mind is racing uncontrollably and bouncing to and fro
Feels like yester year when we were making angels in the snow

Reckless abandon and fearless trust is a must this day and age
I hope all will be well in the coming months and I can smile at this beautiful page

I'll be patient as patient can be without pressure
Continue to be true and honest to allow her to measure

So I'll leave you with this it's a kiss don't dismiss my reason
The fact that all sudden things are good… if only for a season

he loves me not

"to love is to forgive…

and to be able to forgive is a pure blessing in itself"

she loves me

Recapture

Swinging among trees as we did when we were children
Hiding in closets to speak to the one we had a crush on
It's a distant memory of a childish feeling and in adulthood it's all been lost
How grand to recapture the snow fall and the fall of something special
Hold on to this time and grab hold of what's in store
Not taking for granted the time that's been given for whatever reason
It is only in these circumstances that we surrender to happiness
While the rest of the world waits for eternal stretches of joy I'll take mine in moderation
I'll live in the moment as to not forget your face nor your voice
Yes, the sound of the voice, even deeper than the sound of making love
With alluring lunges against the body and the tasting of your sweetness
I'll long for a cosmic wrestle to the finish and the start of a molded clay
You in me and I in you and forged will be the hues of our spirit
Take this chance to feel what I fear you to feel for hope of falling and never waking

he loves me not

"I decided to keep my photo album of long lost loves…

I keep them as a reminder, that he was the end of that…

not the end of me"

she loves me

Beginning and End

You never came around
the night I called you crying
you said you were busy
and you'd see me in the morning

So tell me,
What's her name?
How long has it been since I was unknowingly replaced?

The last tear has fallen and melted into my skin
Just like the sun sets today, your day has come to an end

Don't confuse the end of your life with the beginning of mine

You took advantage of the love I gave and now I'm taking what's mine

Now, don't come asking me to come back because you need me in your life
cause that's where you are confusing the end of yours with the beginning of mine

You took a lot from me
I don't care how much money I spent, that's not what I meant
My love, my hopes, my dreams, and my faith
You took them all and just walked away

But karma is a wonderful thing, you only get out, what you put in
Now, don't mind that I saw her with your brother last night
I'm sure he wasn't aware that you were with his wife

Don't confuse the end of your life with the beginning of mine

It Feels

Love is devastating
It is excruciating
Annihilating
Piercing
Crushing
Cracking
Crumbling
Bamboozling
Complicated
Bitter
Cold
Numbing
Debilitating
Slashing
Vexing
It feels
It feels so fucking good

she loves me

Everyday

I fell asleep feeling your soft kisses
your moist lips
sweet and velvety tongue

I slowly awakened in your arms
warm and tender
safe and content

I went to work with your voice inside my head
The "I love you" and "be safe"
I returned home to a bright smile and a gentle welcome
I came home to my love
my life
my man

I fell again
not to sleep
I fell in love with you again

"stars do not struggle to shine, rivers do not struggle to flow

and you will never struggle to excel in life…

because you deserve the best…

hold on to your dream and it shall be well with you"

she loves me

Sweet Memories

I stare at the moon's face, only to see your face emerge

I listen for the wind, only to hear your laugh in the distance

A few sprinkles of rain fall on my face, and the thought of your touch comes to play

Its sweet, these memories of you

I just have to accept

That's all they will ever be

Sweet memories

he loves me not

Why Bother?

I've flown through many worlds
I've traveled through many a universe
I've swam through the rivers of the milky ways
I've climbed mountains higher than the Himalayas
And yet… I STILL CAN'T REACH YOU

You, who sits in front of me... With whom I lay in bed
The person with whom I have spent my whole life trying to please, trying to show how much you mean to me
I've lost MYSELF in trying to find YOU…
and yet… I STILL CAN'T REACH YOU

I can reach the farthest star in the sky in order to make a wish…
I can reach a shell in the deepest of oceans and listen to the whispers of the mythical mermaids
I can reach the coldest of hearts with my warm soul
and yet… I STILL CAN'T REACH YOU

My arms can no longer stretch as far as they have without being forever ripped away from my material body

My heart can no longer continue beating as much as it has without it literally creating a hole in my chest

I can no longer shed a tear for the pain you have caused me. My eyes, that once upon a time glistened at the thought of you, now are dull… an opaque sheet not letting me see the beauty that still is out there for me

I can no longer reach for something that doesn't want to be captured
I can no longer hold on to holding on
I can no longer wait for you, because in waiting for you to bloom…
I have withered away

she loves me

I have lost myself in trying to find you
I have lost the dreams I dreamed of dreaming of beautiful dreams
for us both… to help me carry on

And now I find myself stuck at a cross road

Do I hurt one by proving my love to the other?
Do I stay and continue to hurt?
Do I hurt everyone in order to feel love?
Or do I just forget me all together and let everyone else be happy?

If you don't want me to find you… then continue hiding
Go ahead and lose yourself… because I still can't reach you… and now, I've forgotten what I was reaching for all along

…Then again… It's not that I have forgotten… rather, I REALIZED... WHY BOTHER?

he loves me not

Alphabetical Reasoning

adoring beautiful charismatic delightful enticing flirty generous heavenly intelligent jolly kind loving mature nurturing optimistic playful quaint respectful sensual tantalizing unique visionary wonderful x… x… x… x… well, she couldn't think of a word that starts with x but the rest are the reasons why she dumped you for that other guy

she loves me

A Real Man Eats…

It is 97°
The room is pitch black
No breeze
The window is wide open but no damn breeze
Couldn't pay the bill so the lights are out hence no fan either
AC? Please
It's all about the fan in the hood
You sure you wanna do this girl?
It's not that I feel bad; it's just that it's so hot
I can't tell if that's sweat or you're already wet
Oh well, I don't care either way
Not because I love you but because I haven't had any in weeks
I know you want me to hurry up and help you get yours but wait
Come here
Sit on the window ledge
Put your leg right here
Damn girl, listen to me, shit! Right here
You wanna do this or you wanna keep complaining about the heat?
Put your leg right here
There you go
You like that?
How about that?
Cool, come to the bed
What?
What the fuck you mean you're done?
Girl that's messed up
I made you bust just by doing that shit?
Girl you're selfish as hell
Take you home?!
Fuck it, next time I'm just gonna bust a nut the first chance I get
And I'm NOT driving your ass home

he loves me not

Until Death Do Us Part

We exchanged the ultimate of decrees
Forever in our hearts etched with a blade like the mighty oak trees

Walking hand in hand into the beginning of our expedition
I'll adore you all the days of my life, you'll see, with no condition

My shoulders will carry the trials that we may encounter
She has been given unto me by Angels and I unto her

Soul to soul and spirit to spirit
We are now one, the glow on our face reveals it

The journey won't be simplistic
Let's make sure that our expectations are realistic

When the mountains become too high to conquer and defeat
It doesn't mean that we've lost and we must retreat

We must refocus our energy and dedication to re-engage
The chapters will never be complete we can always pen an extra page

This path is not for the weak at flesh
The heart is always willing the physical doesn't always mesh

I stood before heaven and hell and announced you as my wife
My loyalty is what you now have, for the rest of my life

she loves me

My Addiction

Her hair flowing with the help of summer breezes
It is my affliction
Her eyes twinkling when she smiles and laughs at my wit
It is my poison
Her skin smooth and golden oh so soft to the touch
It is my toxin
Her voice caressing my senses sweet and gentle
It is my disease
Her lips full and supple silky and delicious
It is my illness
Her love so passionate and engulfing
It is my addiction
…I wish not to be cured

he loves me not

"I guess you can say I live in a fantasy world

I'm in love with the "idea" of falling in love

although I have been through many heartaches…

I don't give up hope in finding that special someone…

remember, that which makes us cry and suffer…

also makes us stronger and wiser"

she loves me

What is Fuck?

Is it something that you say? Is it something that you do? Is it what you think your next door neighbor is? Is it a state of mind? Is it what you'd rather be doing than reading this? Is it really a word? Is what you got when you got cheated on? Is it what you did when you cheated? Is it what you thought you would never let escape your mouth but there you are saying it while you're doing it? Is it what you told your girlfriend when you saw her doing it AND saying it while cheating on you with your best friend? Is it what you did to relieve yourself of that pain? Is it what your neighbors told you to do when they heard you cry at night after doing that because of your now ex girlfriend doing that? Is it what you called the cops on the phone right before you told them what you were going to do because of what she did and you thought that she would never do that with anyone else because she said you were the first person she did that with? Is it near the end because now you can't stop thinking that? Is it what everyone shouted when you told them the story of how you did that and said that while seeing her do that and say that right before you shot them both? Holy shit, I mean fuck.

he loves me not

Drama Momma

Yo momma told you not to date that girl
but you did it anyway
and now your heart is broken

Yo momma told you not to spend all your money on that girl
but you did it anyway
and now you're broke

Yo momma told you not to waste so much time with that girl
but you did it anyway
and now it's too late to register for classes

Yo momma told you not to let your boys hang out with her
but you didn't listen
and now she's pregnant by Carlito

Yo momma told you the baby wasn't yours
but you didn't listen
and now you're trying to explain a dark skinned baby

Yo momma told you to leave her for good
but you didn't listen
and now she's pregnant with your baby too

Yo momma told you she had a dream yo girl wasn't pregnant at all
but you told her she was crazy
and now you got a fat lip
AND
Yo momma was seen hangin out with Carlito

she loves me

"never forget loves from the days gone by…

they are what makes us appreciate what we presently have…

and long for so much more…

amo no porque me ofreces amor…

pero porque se que puedo amar…

amame, y veras"

he loves me not

Home

I knocked on your door but there was no answer
Only the indifference of a jilted cold lover

So many stories, so many memories
All washed away by misunderstanding and miscommunication

The rose bushes are brittle, no longer being watered by your soul
Your eyes glassy and oracle stoned at the sound of my voice

If only holding on a bit longer would make the pain subside
We know that it won't, so we linger in vain

Changing the curtains and the silverware has little to no effect
The root of the chaos still abides in our heart

All that is left is to alter my thinking so that I may find peace
Never wanting to leave her side, for it was truly home

she loves me

"pick flowers, not partners"

he loves me not

"a house is not a home until you cook inside of it…

food is the root of all love"

she loves me

A Third Part of Me

Can you see me?

Can you feel me?

Can you sense my being?

Do you just hear doors closing?

I've been there, standing, sitting, walking, talking, and looking throughout the day and night
However, you have yet to notice

You know I'm here
So why not acknowledge me. Why not accept that I surround you, every waking moment

I inhale your every breathe. Embrace your warmth and speak your words as you pray
Who am I you ask?

Now that you realize you have never been alone, now that you derive a conclusion

Well, if you don't know who I am, how am I supposed to know? You created me, you define me, and you unknowingly acknowledge me and don't even realize it

I am you, as much as you are me, and I, myself, am true to thee
But you hide me. Why?

The "me" you fear, will be taken in jest. Is that why you hid me from the rest?

he loves me not

Nevertheless, here I am, here I lie. Here I will remain and here I will die
Until the day you release the real me within you... that is I

she loves me

"your girlfriend hates you…

she hasn't told you because she loves the shit out of your money"

he loves me not

"D" Batteries

You son of a bitch.
You love me?
You said you what me?
I'm the one you what???
How the fuck are you going to tell me that you "love me" and tell that other skank "I love you"?
Do I look stupid to you? Do you think that for one minute, you could swing that high school player, papi chulo wanna-be, I'm the king of the world Scarface ego shit game, on someone like me? When you thought you were playing me, I was teaching you a lesson.
Yup, you screwed her while you were with me.
Yes, you were seen at the clubs with other women when you were supposedly working longer hours.
Oh yeah, let's not forget the business meetings that ended up being weekend trips to see the tragas you met online.
I applaud you, you got around bitch.
I can only imagine all the "fellas" ruff, ruff, ruff-ing you like crazy.
Now about that lesson… you see, I came out winning.
Now you are alone. No one calls you anymore because they found out the type of player… shit; your "boys" are the ones letting them all know… you know the ones that were cheering you on.
Shit!!! Why not, they are at home with their wives and girlfriends. They cheered you on because you were the only fool willing to fall for their frat style games.
As for me, I'm well… yeah, I'll admit it hurt that you treated me that way. But, hey you know what they say… "Neeeeeeeeext" and your number is up.
Now you are going to miss out on my cooking, my special treatment, my romantic details, and the hot steaming passionate sex you couldn't get enough of.
I've got a whole new life… you see, why would I want you back? All I need are my "D" batteries and I'm set to go.

she loves me

    I'm not spending money on a piece of shit like you. I'm not shedding anymore tears because you chose to be untrue. I'm no longer suffering and wondering where the hell you are, who you have been with, or what you have been doing.
    Nah… just recharge dem dere batteries and I'm all good.

he loves me not

What's it Like?

Love is like dying and being given another chance to live.
It's like seeing the truth in someone's eyes and not have a reason to second guess them.
It's like walking on a warm day and feeling that soft little drizzle of rain that revives your senses.
It's being around him without physically being in front of him.
It's reading a poem in a book and giggling because you feel someone just read your journal and liked your entry so much that they felt the need to print it on a card and share it with the world.
It's sleeping with one of his dress shirts that still has his cologne sprayed on it.
It's living the most fabulous fantasy ever imaginable. You know, the one your brain started master minding since the moment you first kissed but never told him.
It's honoring the sacrifices he makes for you and accepting that although he may not be perfect… he's the closest thing to perfection.
It's that feeling of joy because he accepts you for who you are and not what he wants you to be… because after all, you are all he ever needs.
It's the little things, the serenades (off key), and the little notes he leaves for you on your pillow that say "Wish I was here".
It's the feel of his hands rubbing your shoulders when you are having a bad day and the soft gentle sincerity of his voice saying "It's going to be alright babe… I'm here for you".
It's that call you get when he's out of town telling you that "If you can see the moon, then I'm never too far away".
Love is just that… love. Unconditional, indescribable, unprecedented, truth, respect, and trust.
In all its simplicity. It's simply marvelous.

she loves me

I am an author/writer, film maker, designer, philanthropist, manager, organizer, publisher, President, CEO, Founder, Chairman, artist, thinker, listener, son, brother, friend, loyalist, bodyguard, enforcer, counselor, mentor, ref, lover, fighter, patriot, jibaro, entrepreneur, inventor, poet, and dreamer...and yet none of this defines who I am. God's purpose in my life is bigger than anything I can ever imagine

he loves me not

If you look for me and I am nowhere to be found, look up at the
sky, I will be the first star to the left of the moon that you see
Tell me your dreams, tell me your sorrows
I will always be listening

she loves me

love deeply

♥